UnDiet Your Mind: Eat with Ease

Jenna Free & Lauren McAulay

Copyright © 2021 The Body Love Society

ISBN: 9798755053969

DEDICATION

This journal is dedicated to every UnDieter doing the work to change diet culture by healing their own relationship with food and their body. You are making a difference!

WELCOME

Welcome to UnDiet Your Mind: Eat with Ease

This is a powerful 60 day journal to begin UnDieting your mind so you can think about food differently. This will allow you to begin healing from dieting, binge eating, food obsession and you'll become stronger every day in your Intuitive Eating Skills just by changing the way you think about food.

We are Jenna Free and Lauren McAulay, Intuitive Eating Counselors who have worked with people all over the world in repairing their relationships with food and their bodies. We were chronic dieters ourselves for over 10 years, binge ate regularly and felt completely obsessed with food. It wasn't until we began exploring UnDieting that we began to heal.

UnDieting means unlearning the beliefs, 'information', and habits that diet culture has taught us over the years. We were taught that we should be constantly pursuing weight loss, that we should all be in thin bodies and that food is something to be restricted and obsessively tracked.

And all that landed us here:

- Obsessed with food (maybe even feeling addicted)

- Always on or off a diet

- Feeling guilty about eating even when we aren't on a diet

- Stuck in the cycle of restricting and bingeing (all or nothing)

- Never feeling good enough

So how do we unlearn these things?

An effective path to unlearning is repetition and consistency of a new message and that is exactly what you get to do in this journal!

It takes time and repetition to build new neural pathways but it doesn't have to be hard! Just come back to this journal each day (or as often as you can).

Building new beliefs and ways of thinking about food will change your life and you'll notice yourself eating differently without consciously trying to.

Imagine:

- Having whatever food you want in the house and you just enjoy it when you feel like it

- Never having to diet and feeling good physically

- Feeling at peace around food

- Taking care of your body but in a way that is actually enjoyable and sustainable

- Never having to follow any food rules ever again (yes, you CAN trust your body)

This is all possible with UnDieting and unlearning all of the toxic beliefs that diet culture bestowed to us.

HOW IT WORKS:

Each day open your journal up and do 1 day of journaling.

Each day comes with one journal prompt (designed to have you start thinking differently about food and eating) and a set of daily check in questions.

The daily questions are simple check ins to see how you're feeling.

The questions are:

1. Today I am feeling _____. *This allows you to let it out, suppressing emotions never helps.*

2. Today I am happy about/ proud of/ grateful for/ finding peace with _____. (circle one). *This allows you to remember the good in your life even on a hard day.*

3. Today I want to focus on _____. *For this question you can choose your own focus or you can use one of ours. These are specific skills or ideas that you want to work on today. If you just think about one small area a day to work on it will be much more manageable and you'll actually do it!*

Areas you can focus on:

- Tasting each bite of my food

- Being present when eating my meals

- Identifying when I'm hungry

- Identifying when I'm full

- Allowing what I want to eat freely

- Noticing any food rules that come up

- Not overthinking what to eat, just eat and move on

- Being satisfied each time I eat (feeling done!)

- Not labeling food as good and bad

- Allowing carbs at every meal

- Allowing dessert if I want it (#lunchdessert)

- Eating before work so I don't get overly hungry

- Adding spices, butters and flavor to meals to make them more enjoyable
- Noticing my thoughts around food

These daily focuses can be large or small but choosing one a day can help move things along much faster than just trying to "listen to your body", that's too vague and overwhelming to really do anything with.

That's it!

Show up each day, take ten minutes to do your journaling and you'll find yourself starting to think differently about food.

There is also a spot for daily notes. Becoming more aware of why we eat how we do, why we think about food the way we do and why we disparage our bodies the way we do (hint: it all stems from the beliefs that diet culture gave us) is a major part of healing.

Whenever you have an a-ha moment or notice something, jot it down.

In dieting we just go through the motions and we rarely question what we're doing. It's time for that to stop.

PS - You'll also see a daily affirmation on the bottom of every day's journaling. xo

Have questions? Reach out to us anytime at hello@thebodylovesociety.com.

DAY 1
DATE _____

Today I am feeling:

Today I am happy about/ proud of/ grateful for/ finding peace with:

Today I want to focus on:

Notes:

"No matter what I ate yesterday, I still get to eat what I desire today."

First you need to declare your why. This work can be tough at times so this will be a reminder of what you're working towards.

Describe what your life would look like and what you would do differently if you were free around food and felt at home in your body (even if your body didn't change physically)?

DAY 2
DATE _____

Today I am feeling:

Today I am happy about/ proud of/ grateful for/ finding peace with:

Today I want to focus on:

Notes:

"When I feel overwhelmed, I give myself compassion."

Let's focus on the positives that food brings into our lives instead of always focusing on the fears around it.

Write out 5+ positive things that food contributes to your life.

Examples: enjoying dinners out with friends, tastes great, allows you to satisfy hunger.

DAY 3
DATE _____

Today I am feeling:

Today I am happy about/ proud of/ grateful for/ finding peace with:

Today I want to focus on:

Notes:

"When I accept my body it gives others permission to do the same"

What are 1-3 foods that you would like to feel more free around?

Let's look into why you might not be feeling free around these foods.

Do you eat this food rarely/special occasions (this can include only eating it at night when you're alone)?

Do you feel bad about eating this food?

Do you try to only eat small amounts or limit yourself when eating this food?

Do you eat it all just to get it out of the house/ not be tempted by having leftovers?

If you answered yes to any of these questions you likely have a scarcity mindset around this food.

Start with one food and let's get abundant!

1. Get the food in the house
2. Eat it at various times in the day
3. When you eat it reassure yourself that this food is part of normal eating

DAY 4
DATE _____

Today I am feeling:

Today I am happy about/ proud of/ grateful for/ finding peace with:

Today I want to focus on:

Notes:

"I make empowered choices. When I make a decision, I own it!"

If diet culture did not exist, what would you think of food? How would you relate to food?

How would you think about and relate to your body?

DAY 5
DATE _____

Today I am feeling:

Today I am happy about/ proud of/ grateful for/ finding peace with:

Today I want to focus on:

Notes:

" I am always doing enough"

What are the most enjoyable parts of allowing yourself to eat what you want and not be on a meal plan anymore?

DAY 6
DATE _____

Today I am feeling:

Today I am happy about/ proud of/ grateful for/ finding peace with:

Today I want to focus on:

Notes:

"I get to choose my own beliefs and values. Just because our society values something doesn't mean I have to."

When was the last time you felt really full or binge ate? What feelings do you have about this past experience?

Now, how can you give yourself compassion and take judgment out of it? What would be helpful to hear if this situation happens again?

DAY 7
DATE _____

Today I am feeling:

Today I am happy about/ proud of/ grateful for/ finding peace with:

Today I want to focus on:

Notes:

"No is a complete sentence."

Think about your meals the last few days. Do you feel nourished? If not what would you like to shift?

Remember: Nourishment is about ADDING, never restriction.

DAY 8
DATE _____

Today I am feeling:

Today I am happy about/ proud of/ grateful for/ finding peace with:

Today I want to focus on:

Notes:

"All bodies are good bodies"

Think of a food that you think is "bad" (or used to think was "bad"). Brainstorm some things that are GOOD about this food.

(Let's start easing away from all or nothing thinking).

DAY 9
DATE _____

Today I am feeling:

Today I am happy about/ proud of/ grateful for/ finding peace with:

Today I want to focus on:

Notes:

"Eating is meant to be pleasurable. I will enjoy my food today."

Satisfaction is an important aspect of healing your relationship with food. It means feeling truly done after eating. For many this might mean something sweet after dinner or including carbs in their meals.

Describe what it feels like to be satisfied after you eat. How often do you experience this? How can you experience this more often?

And what does it feel like to not be satisfied, what happens when you don't feel done after eating?

DAY 10
DATE _____

Today I am feeling:

Today I am happy about/ proud of/ grateful for/ finding peace with:

Today I want to focus on:

Notes:

"Being outside of my comfort zone is how I will grow."

Share about your latest great food experience. Share about the food, the situation, what was great about it, how do you see your relationship with food changing?

DAY 11
DATE _____

Today I am feeling:

Today I am happy about/ proud of/ grateful for/ finding peace with:

Today I want to focus on:

Notes:

"The purpose of hunger is to cue me to eat. I can safely listen to those signals"

What is one food you're still preoccupied with?

What if this is the only food you could eat for the rest of your life? How does this change your thoughts on this food?

This is the power of allowing! (Although the point is not to get sick of the food but just to normalize it and release the power it has).

DAY 12
DATE _____

Today I am feeling:

Today I am happy about/ proud of/ grateful for/ finding peace with:

Today I want to focus on:

Notes:

"My body is exactly the way it's meant to be right now."

What are your biggest fears in letting yourself allow all food?

How likely are these fears to come true?

What is a more likely, more realistic scenario?

DAY 13
DATE _____

Today I am feeling:

Today I am happy about/ proud of/ grateful for/ finding peace with:

Today I want to focus on:

Notes:

"My body and I are on the same team."

It can be enticing, at times, to go back to dieting or even just limiting things in a "sensible" way. But let's reflect on your previous experience with restriction and dieting.

What happens when you restrict? Short term? Long term?

DAY 14
DATE _____

Today I am feeling:

Today I am happy about/ proud of/ grateful for/ finding peace with:

Today I want to focus on:

Notes:

"Food is not good or bad. Food is just food!"

At the end of your life what will matter most to you - how you lived your life or how your body looked?

How can you prioritize the important things NOW that you know will matter most at the end of your life?

DAY 15
DATE _____

Today I am feeling:

Today I am happy about/ proud of/ grateful for/ finding peace with:

Today I want to focus on:

Notes:

"Convenience foods have a place in my life and I never have to feel bad for that."

What feels hard with UnDieting currently? Give a voice to the hard parts of this work.

How can you get the support to make it feel less hard?

DAY 16
DATE _____

Today I am feeling:

Today I am happy about/ proud of/ grateful for/ finding peace with:

Today I want to focus on:

Notes:

"My weight is not my worth."

If a child asked you the difference between an apple and a cookie, what would your response be (using an UnDiet narrative)?

Your response is how you get to speak to yourself.

DAY 17
DATE _____

Today I am feeling:

Today I am happy about/ proud of/ grateful for/ finding peace with:

Today I want to focus on:

Notes:

"My body is the least interesting thing about me."

To date, what is the most freeing experience you have had with food?

DAY 18
DATE _____

Today I am feeling:

Today I am happy about/ proud of/ grateful for/ finding peace with:

Today I want to focus on:

Notes:

"Presence is my power!"

Presence is vital in Intuitive Eating.

How can you be more present today?
How can you be more present with food?
How about in your life in general?

DAY 19
DATE _____

Today I am feeling:

Today I am happy about/ proud of/ grateful for/ finding peace with:

Today I want to focus on:

Notes:

"I deserve to feel free and at peace with food and my body."

Let's practice listening to your body.
Tune in right now - what do you feel?
Describe everything from your feet to your head.

DAY 20
DATE _____

Today I am feeling:

Today I am happy about/ proud of/ grateful for/ finding peace with:

Today I want to focus on:

Notes:

"Happiness does not come in the form of a pant size."

Be spontaneous with food today. Is it a pizza night? A dinner with your friends? Eating lunch out instead of what you planned to pack?

How spontaneous have you been with food in the past?

How can you fit spontaneity into your meals?

DAY 21
DATE _____

Today I am feeling:

Today I am happy about/ proud of/ grateful for/ finding peace with:

Today I want to focus on:

Notes:

"Whatever I'm doing, it's always enough."

People often think that dieting is a way to "stay in control." But in reality we cannot control our bodies.

How can you release some control with food?
In your life?

DAY 22
DATE _____

Today I am feeling:

Today I am happy about/ proud of/ grateful for/ finding peace with:

Today I want to focus on:

Notes:

"Even if I don't like my body, I can always respect it."

Write down your dream day (and the role food has in it). How do you feel in your body during this day?

DAY 23
DATE _____

Today I am feeling:

Today I am happy about/ proud of/ grateful for/ finding peace with:

Today I want to focus on:

Notes:

"I am healing and transforming my relationship with food and my body. Even when it feels hard, it'll be worth it."

Part of the healing process with food is having an abundant mindset.

What feelings come up for you when you imagine having a fear food in your house in abundance?
What do you think will happen if you allow yourself to stock up (instead of living in scarcity)?

What good can come from living in food abundance?

DAY 24
DATE _____

Today I am feeling:

Today I am happy about/ proud of/ grateful for/ finding peace with:

Today I want to focus on:

Notes:

"I am whole and I belong."

All or nothing thinking is one of the most damaging mindsets in dieting. We're either being "perfect" or saying screw it!

When was the last time you had an experience with all or nothing thinking with food?

How could you have had more balanced thinking in this specific situation?

DAY 25
DATE _____

Today I am feeling:

Today I am happy about/ proud of/ grateful for/ finding peace with:

Today I want to focus on:

Notes:

"Every day I'm not dieting is one day closer to food freedom!"

Fullness is demonized in dieting and it can be hard to begin allowing yourself to get truly full when you eat.

In UnDieting, allowing yourself to get full is a good thing. It provides satisfaction, reduces food preoccupation and allows you to go longer between meals (beneficial for those who have a busy schedule and can't make time to eat every couple of hours).

What benefits do you see in letting yourself be full?

DAY 26
DATE _____

Today I am feeling:

Today I am happy about/ proud of/ grateful for/ finding peace with:

Today I want to focus on:

Notes:

"I can do hard things."

What are 5 foods that honor your body and what are the reasons that they are self honoring?

(Try for a mix of foods that you previously saw as "good" and "bad", this will reveal that there is a place for ALL foods).

DAY 27
DATE _____

Today I am feeling:

Today I am happy about/ proud of/ grateful for/ finding peace with:

Today I want to focus on:

Notes:

"Acceptance is not complacency, it's learning to be okay with reality."

What signs and signals tell you that you're hungry?
*They are different for everyone.

How do you usually respond to these signals?

DAY 28
DATE _____

Today I am feeling:

Today I am happy about/ proud of/ grateful for/ finding peace with:

Today I want to focus on:

Notes:

"I eat with ease. I can just eat and move on with my day."

How do the people around you affect how you eat?
If your friends all order a salad do you feel the need to do the same?
Are you conscious of eating more than your partner?

How can you create more autonomy with your eating?
Are you willing to begin listening to YOUR body and not let others sway your food choices?

DAY 29
DATE _____

Today I am feeling:

Today I am happy about/ proud of/ grateful for/ finding peace with:

Today I want to focus on:

Notes:

"I listen to my body and honor my cravings."

Do you judge your body signals?
Which ones are you judgemental of?
Why do you think that is?

DAY 30
DATE _____

Today I am feeling:

Today I am happy about/ proud of/ grateful for/ finding peace with:

Today I want to focus on:

Notes:

"Weight does not equal health. I define my own health!"

What is one food experience that happened recently that you judged?
What did you not like about it?

How could you learn from it instead?

DAY 31
DATE _____

Today I am feeling:

Today I am happy about/ proud of/ grateful for/ finding peace with:

Today I want to focus on:

Notes:

"I can practice health at any size."

When you eat, what fills your thoughts?
Can you spot any diet mentality?
You can do this while eating a meal today.

Having awareness will help you start to shift the diet mentality to the UnDiet mentality.

DAY 32
DATE _____

Today I am feeling:

Today I am happy about/ proud of/ grateful for/ finding peace with:

Today I want to focus on:

Notes:

"I make self honoring choices, there is never a wrong answer."

If your relationship with food and your body were completely healed, what would you put your energy towards?

What gets to come into your life after the food and body obsession has faded?

DAY 33
DATE _____

Today I am feeling:

Today I am happy about/ proud of/ grateful for/ finding peace with:

Today I want to focus on:

Notes:

"I move my body in ways that feel good to me."

If you had one meal left to eat, what would it be?

What thoughts would you have while eating this meal knowing it would be your last?

Would there be any diet mentality or judgment involved? Or would you completely allow yourself to choose what you want and relish in it?

If anything, what is stopping you from allowing and enjoying your food as you did if it were your last meal?

DAY 34
DATE _____

Today I am feeling:

Today I am happy about/ proud of/ grateful for/ finding peace with:

Today I want to focus on:

Notes:

"I am a strong and confident person!"

If you could have a dinner party with anyone, who would you invite? What food would be served? What conversation would you like to have with them?

How would this experience be changed if you were stressed about what to eat at this dinner?

DAY 35

DATE _____

Today I am feeling:

Today I am happy about/ proud of/ grateful for/ finding peace with:

Today I want to focus on:

Notes:

"It's okay to feel ALL of my feelings, the light and the dark."

How does it make you feel to know that you can eat dessert on any day of the week and any time of day?

What feels scary about that?

What feels liberating about that?

DAY 36
DATE _____

Today I am feeling:

Today I am happy about/ proud of/ grateful for/ finding peace with:

Today I want to focus on:

Notes:

"A healthy body image is not about the size of my body, it's about the thoughts and beliefs inside my mind."

Reflect on the things that have improved since starting your UnDiet Journey.

*It's so easy to only see how far we have left to go and we ignore how far we've come!

DAY 37
DATE _____

Today I am feeling:

Today I am happy about/ proud of/ grateful for/ finding peace with:

Today I want to focus on:

Notes:

"I don't compare myself to others, I stay in my own lane."

How are the holidays and special occasions different now that you are working through the process of becoming an UnDieter?

What stresses come up for you around special occasions as an UnDieter?

What things feel easier and more fun?

DAY 38
DATE _____

Today I am feeling:

Today I am happy about/ proud of/ grateful for/ finding peace with:

Today I want to focus on:

Notes:

"I speak positively about myself."

Is there anything you still feel like you force yourself into doing that you don't authentically or intuitively want to do but diet culture still has that "hold" over you?

What are these things?

What would happen if you stopped doing these things/ did less of it?

DAY 39
DATE _____

Today I am feeling:

Today I am happy about/ proud of/ grateful for/ finding peace with:

Today I want to focus on:

Notes:

"Just because the world applauds weight loss doesn't mean it's the answer."

If you could make our society believe new things about bodies and food what would they be?

What new culture would you create?

Now THESE are your true beliefs. How can you incorporate these thoughts and ideas into how you think about YOUR body?

DAY 40

DATE _____

Today I am feeling:

Today I am happy about/ proud of/ grateful for/ finding peace with:

Today I want to focus on:

Notes:

"When I show up as my authentic self, I inspire others to do the same."

When was the last time you sat down with a meal and had no distractions?

How does it change things when you're less distracted while eating?

What came up for you here? Was it that being less distracted means you probably will be more tuned in and eat less and that's a good thing?

What UnDiet reasons might there be to try to be less distracted when eating? (Also, the choice to not care about this completely valid!)

DAY 41
DATE _____

Today I am feeling:

Today I am happy about/ proud of/ grateful for/ finding peace with:

Today I want to focus on:

Notes:

"I pay attention to the way I FEEL in my body."

Today we're going to try some stream of consciousness writing.

Write down all your thoughts about where you're at with food and your body as they come to you, without stopping or editing.

DAY 42
DATE _____

Today I am feeling:

Today I am happy about/ proud of/ grateful for/ finding peace with:

Today I want to focus on:

Notes:

"I give myself the same love and kindness I do to my inner child."

When were you first told that weight loss was good, that certain foods were bad and that weight equals health?

Do you remember anything from before you believed these things?

If yes, what was that like? If no, what do you think that would have been like?

DAY 43
DATE _____

Today I am feeling:

Today I am happy about/ proud of/ grateful for/ finding peace with:

Today I want to focus on:

Notes:

"I am free to be myself."

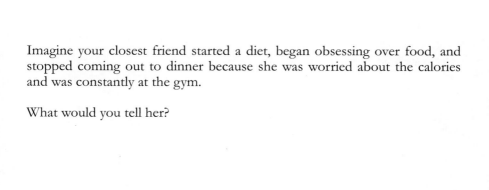

Imagine your closest friend started a diet, began obsessing over food, and stopped coming out to dinner because she was worried about the calories and was constantly at the gym.

What would you tell her?

*These words are really for yourself. If you don't think a friend needs to be doing this to change their body then neither do you!

DAY 44

DATE _____

Today I am feeling:

Today I am happy about/ proud of/ grateful for/ finding peace with:

Today I want to focus on:

Notes:

"I have an abundant mindset with food!"

Create a therapeutic cooking experience.

Find a fun new recipe, pour yourself a glass of wine/mocktail, and put on your favorite music or podcast.

What would it be like to prioritize time in your day to give yourself this experience with food? What would feel good about this experience? What may deter you from wanting to try out this experience? Reflect below.

When completed, reflect on what this experience was like for you.

DAY 45
DATE _____

Today I am feeling:

Today I am happy about/ proud of/ grateful for/ finding peace with:

Today I want to focus on:

Notes:

"I prioritize my self-care."

We need to consistently remind ourselves of what is possible if we can let go of the diet mentality ...

If you could travel anywhere in the world, where would you go? What would the experience be like without having to worry about any food or body concerns?

DAY 46
DATE _____

Today I am feeling:

Today I am happy about/ proud of/ grateful for/ finding peace with:

Today I want to focus on:

Notes:

"I honor my hunger and allow myself to eat when I need to (and also when I want to)."

What are 5 things you can do or adjust if you aren't feeling good in your body that aren't focused on weight or restricting food?

DAY 47
DATE _____

Today I am feeling:

Today I am happy about/ proud of/ grateful for/ finding peace with:

Today I want to focus on:

Notes:

"I give myself compassion even on the days that challenge me."

How do you feel when you listen to your body and get into the groove of intuitive eating?

How does it feel both physically and mentally?

If you haven't experienced this yet, what do you imagine it feels like?

Remind yourself of these feelings in any tough moments.

DAY 48
DATE _____

Today I am feeling:

Today I am happy about/ proud of/ grateful for/ finding peace with:

Today I want to focus on:

Notes:

"I eat food that satisfies me without judgement."

Eating nutrient dense food does not mean it has to taste bland. Have you explored adding butters, sauces, dressings, oils, spices?

Is there something you find that you really enjoy now that you know you can add taste?

Write down anything you want to try or have appreciated now that you're more flexible with your eating.

DAY 49
DATE _____

Today I am feeling:

Today I am happy about/ proud of/ grateful for/ finding peace with:

Today I want to focus on:

Notes:

"I set boundaries that keep me feeling safe and supported. I also can get out of my comfort zone when needed."

What is your first initial reaction when you have a craving for something?

What would it feel like to just allow yourself to eat what you are craving without any judgment and move on?

DAY 50
DATE _____

Today I am feeling:

Today I am happy about/ proud of/ grateful for/ finding peace with:

Today I want to focus on:

Notes:

"I find pleasure and joy in food! It's a fun part of life."

Being the "teacher" will strengthen your UnDieting abilities.

What advice would you give someone who is just starting to UnDiet?

DAY 51

DATE _____

Today I am feeling:

Today I am happy about/ proud of/ grateful for/ finding peace with:

Today I want to focus on:

Notes:

"I'm safe to eat and feel my fullness."

What food did you enjoy eating as a child?

What would it be like to eat this food today?

Do you think you would be able to allow yourself to enjoy it just like you did when you were a child who knew nothing of diet culture yet? If not, what is standing in your way?

DAY 52
DATE _____

Today I am feeling:

Today I am happy about/ proud of/ grateful for/ finding peace with:

Today I want to focus on:

Notes:

"It's okay to NOT always feel good in my body, it can ebb and flow."

If you choose not to eat the cookie you were offered that's okay! You don't always have to say yes to food.

BUT it's important to check in with WHY you didn't eat the cookie. Is it because you felt like you "shouldn't" or your body genuinely didn't think it would feel good?

When was the last time you skipped eating something? Why? Check in with that intention behind the decision.

How does not eating something because you're listening to your body feel different than not eating something because you don't allow yourself?

DAY 53
DATE _____

Today I am feeling:

Today I am happy about/ proud of/ grateful for/ finding peace with:

Today I want to focus on:

Notes:

"I release the need to control the size of my body. I am safe to be in the body I have today."

The type of energy you feel when eating makes a difference.

Imagine you are eating a cookie with guilt. Describe how that experience would feel, what thoughts would you have, how fast would you eat? Describe as much as you can.

Now, imagine you are eating a cookie with joy and free of judgement. Describe how the experience would feel.

What are strategies you can come up with that will allow you to eat with joyful and non-judgmental energy when you are eating?

DAY 54
DATE _____

Today I am feeling:

Today I am happy about/ proud of/ grateful for/ finding peace with:

Today I want to focus on:

Notes:

"I listen to my body when it needs rest."

If you completely trusted your body how would you eat differently, move differently and treat your body differently?

DAY 55
DATE _____

Today I am feeling:

Today I am happy about/ proud of/ grateful for/ finding peace with:

Today I want to focus on:

Notes:

"The most powerful thing someone can say to me is what I say to myself." -Christine D'Ercole

At this moment, what thoughts and feelings do you have about food?

Which thoughts feel like yours and which are coming from diet culture?

DAY 56
DATE _____

Today I am feeling:

Today I am happy about/ proud of/ grateful for/ finding peace with:

Today I want to focus on:

Notes:

" I never need to fear my favorite foods, I can enjoy them freely."

Imagine a friend came to you and said, "I binged last night and feel so upset. I feel so ashamed."

What would you tell them? How would you support them?

DAY 57
DATE _____

Today I am feeling:

Today I am happy about/ proud of/ grateful for/ finding peace with:

Today I want to focus on:

Notes:

"I wake up each day and do my best. Whatever I do, is enough."

Do you notice any judgments that you have about others when you see them eating or buying food at the grocery store?

Where do these judgements come from - your true self or diet culture?

What could you shift these judgements to if this happens again? (HINT: neutral thoughts are a great place to start).

DAY 58
DATE _____

Today I am feeling:

Today I am happy about/ proud of/ grateful for/ finding peace with:

Today I want to focus on:

Notes:

"I use curiosity over judgement."

Is there any kind of food that feels nostalgic? What kinds of food feel this way for you?

What feelings do these foods bring up in you?

How are these foods altered if you're stressing about the calories etc?

DAY 59
DATE _____

Today I am feeling:

Today I am happy about/ proud of/ grateful for/ finding peace with:

Today I want to focus on:

Notes:

"I look for things in life that I appreciate and feel grateful for."

What are 3-5 things that you are struggling with in your relationship with food still?

What would happen if instead of constantly trying to fix these things, you began to learn to accept them (this doesn't mean it'll never change)?

Sit with this idea: that you can accept the parts of your relationship with food that aren't where you want them to be yet. Does this provide any sort of relief?

Please note: accepting does not mean it'll never change and you can't work on it but it provides space for self compassion WHILE you're working on healing.

DAY 60
DATE _____

Today I am feeling:

Today I am happy about/ proud of/ grateful for/ finding peace with:

Today I want to focus on:

Notes:

"Life is not about reaching a destination, it's about learning and growing and living each day to the fullest."

Where do you feel you are at in your process with UnDieting your mind?

What has been going well?

What transformation have you noticed?

What is something you'd like to continue to work through?

Congratulations!

You have completed the UnDiet Your Mind: Eat with Ease journal.

This means you have sat down and worked on your relationship with food 60 times, that is an amazing feat.

Every time we give our brain new perspectives to consider, we get one step closer to creating new thoughts and beliefs around food (and our bodies).

What are your next steps?

That depends, what kind of support do you want moving forward?

You can learn more about your options such as the UnDiet Your Mind App, Step by Step courses, 1:1 coaching and more at thebodylovesociety.com.

If you aren't sure what to do next you can also email us hello@thebodylovesociety.com.

ABOUT THE AUTHORS

Lauren McAulay and Jenna Free are Intuitive Eating Counsellors and soon to be therapists from Los Angeles and Calgary, AB respectively. They have worked with hundreds of people, all over the world in repairing their relationships with food and their bodies. They are co-founders of The Body Love Society and have created many resources to help you UnDiet Your Mind and find peace with food and your body. Be sure to check out their app, courses, coaching services, other published books and more!

Get more information at thebodylovesociety.com

Made in United States
North Haven, CT
25 March 2022

17513349R00072